SCARBOROUGH RAILWAY STA
FROM STEAM AGE TO DIESEL ERA

A Pictorial Record of a Seaside Railway Terminus

By J. Robin Lidster

author of

'*The Scarborough & Whitby Railway*', '*The Forge Valley Line*', '*Railway Posters of the Yorkshire Coast*', '*Robin Hood's Bay As It Was*' etc.

1. *Scarborough from the Seamer Road* a lithograph of about 1850 showing the approach to the town with the five-arch bridge and an early train in the centre.

Scarborough Public Library.

Published by Hendon Publishing Co. Ltd., Hendon Mill, Nelson, Lancashire.
© J. Robin Lidster, 1995
Printed by Fretwell Print And Design Ltd., Goulbourne Street, Keighley, West Yorkshire

INTRODUCTION

Plans for a railway from York to Malton and Scarborough were mooted as early as 1833 but nothing materialised until 1840. In this year a survey was completed under the direction of Sir John Rennie for a railway from Scarborough harbour to a junction with the York & North Midland Railway near York. A similar plan was deposited with the authorities on 1 March 1841. On 1 March 1842 another plan was deposited for a scheme for a York, Malton & Scarborough Railway with a branch to join the then independent Whitby & Pickering line at Pickering. On 30 November 1843 plans were deposited for a railway to commence by a junction with the York & North Midland Railway and the Great North of England Railway, or one of them, near the City of York. This was the scheme which had the backing and the interest of the chairman of the Y&NMR, George Hudson, and the engineer for this scheme was Robert Stephenson.

The proposals to bring the railway to Scarborough were not met with great enthusiasm by all the inhabitants of the town, in particular George Knowles, of Wood End, who published a pamphlet on 1 January 1844 in which he remonstrated in great detail, and at great length, against a railway coming to Scarborough.

Knowles quoted George Hudson as saying that he had no doubt of Scarborough becoming the 'Brighton of the North' and that he considered Scarborough so much improved that he called it the 'Queen of Watering Places' – a title which was to remain current in railway advertising for the resort for the next eighty years and is still a familiar phrase today, 150 years after it was first coined. Knowles went on to state that – 'A railroad has been of no service to Brighton as a watering place . . . it has had the effect of driving several families to Scarborough who used to spend their summer months there.' He concluded that this was a bad omen and suggested that the railway would substitute a class of visitors who had much to gain and little or nothing to spend. The result, he suggested, would be that Scarborough would have to submit to a very considerable increase in its poor rates, and also to the expense of a more extensive building for the accommodation of paupers, as well as to an enlargement of the jail(sic), for confining a greater number of thieves, pickpockets and vagrants, which a railway would most certainly entail upon them – then this 'Queen of Watering Places' would have to weep over her fallen greatness and rue the day she ever saw her shores invaded by a railroad!

It was fortunate for the development of Scarborough as a seaside resort that the views of George Knowles were not too widely accepted although some residents may well think that some of his prophesies have come about! There is no doubt that Scarborough owes her present position as the east coast's premier seaside resort (a position albeit somewhat tarnished due to lack of maintenance and capital investment in recent years) to the building of the railway.

Construction of the line took only about twelve months although some preliminary work had been undertaken prior to July 1844. Apart from negotiating Kirkham Gorge, just to the south-west of Malton, the land through which the line passes was relatively level and there were no major engineering works between York and Scarborough. There were only 25 bridges in the 42 mile line, the two largest being the bridge over the River Ouse at York and the five arch Washbeck viaduct at Scarborough.

The official opening took place on Monday 7 July 1845 when an inaugural train of thirty-five coaches, hauled by two engines, *Hudson* and *Lion*, brought a large party from York, arriving in Scarborough at about 1-35 p.m. having taken just over three hours, with stops at Castle Howard, Malton and Ganton. At Scarborough all the shops were closed and it was estimated that between ten and fifteen thousand spectators witnessed the arrival of the train.

Speeches were made by the Mayor of Scarborough, Thomas Weddell and the Director of the York & North Midland Railway Company, George Hudson, in one of the rooms at the station, after which 'the company retired in sections to partake of Luncheon, which was served up by Mrs Reed upon the platform

2. A watercolour sketch of Scarborough station in the 1850s showing a double-headed train in the snow.   Author's Collection.

3. An illustration from the billhead of a Scarborough tallow chandler (candle maker) showing the front elevation of the original station before the extensive alterations of the 1880s. Author's Collection.

at the end of the station, a temporary roof having been erected for the occasion'.

After the luncheon, and the customary speeches and responses, the party formed a procession to walk through the town accompanied by a band of musicians. A contemporary account reports that – 'Close upon the station a most prominent and very beautiful object presented itself – a triumphal arch, constructed in accordance with the strictest principles of architecture and very richly decorated. It occupies the entire width of the York road and was surmounted with a flag bearing the words – "Long Live The Queen". Across the centre of the arch was inscribed this dedication – "To Geo. Hudson Esq., and the Directors of the York and Scarborough Railway". On the piers of the arch were emblazoned the arms of York and Scarborough.' The procession proceeded through the arch, to the Bar, down Newborough Street, along St Nicholas Street, past the beautiful Elizabethan mansion of John Woodall, and then back to the station by way of Huntriss Row. The return trip to York, augmented by the Corporation of Scarborough and other invited guests, departed from Scarborough at 3-45 p.m.

In an account of the opening of the line in the *Yorkshire Gazette* of 12 July 1845 (also quoted above) the station is described as being – 'of stone, and in some respects not unlike the York Station (at that time the small station was within the city walls). It *will* have a wrought iron and glazed roof 348 feet long by 88 feet wide in two spans and 30 feet from the rails to the skylight. The refreshment rooms are quite as extensive as those at York and more handsome. The buildings, designed by Mr G. T. Andrews, of York, are in the Italian style, and have a beautiful colonnade in front (see photograph 3).

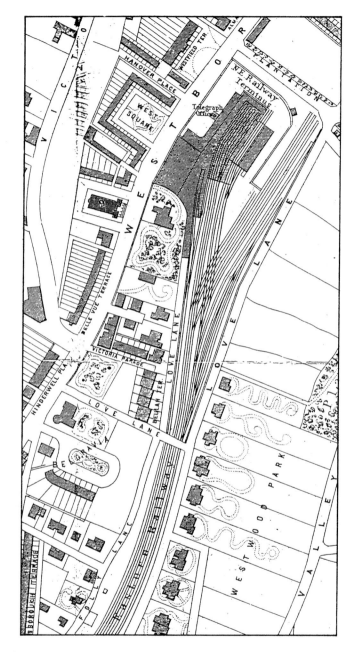

4. A semi-diagrammatic plan of the station, taken from a town map by S. W. Theakston, published in the 1870s.

Author's Collection.

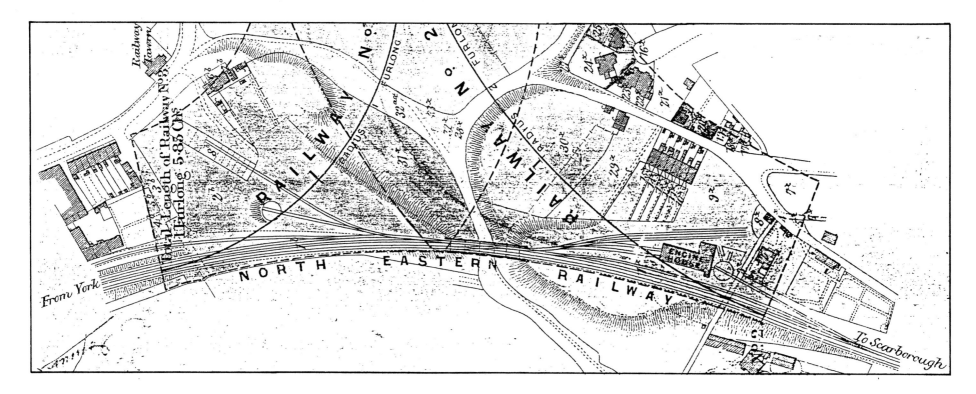

5. This drawing, which is a small detail taken from the deposited plans of the Scarborough & Whitby Railway of 1865, shows the proposed junction of that line with the North Eastern Railway at Falsgrave. It also shows some interesting details of the layout as it existed at that time. The old Engine House and turntable can be seen at the eastern end and, just above, the terrace which is still called Locomotive Cottages. In the centre of the drawing is the five-arch bridge, originally known as Washbeck Viaduct, which was demolished in the 1880s. It was replaced by a wider, single span bridge, but is still known by some local people as 'five-arches'. At the west end of the site, later known as Falsgrave sidings, is a small goods yard with coal drops and another turntable. When the new engine shed, a roundhouse, was built adjacent to Seamer Road / Seamer Street in 1881 the Engine House was converted to a goods depot and this site was chosen for the new excursion station which opened in 1908.

Author's Collection.

6. This illustration, from an old magic lantern slide, shows the area covered by the eastern end of the plan, above. The old Engine House, a goods depot by the time the photograph was taken, and the Locomotive Cottages, can be seen in the centre of the photograph.

Author's Collection.

The waiting rooms and booking offices are all on one floor, and there *will* be warehouses for heavy goods, merchandise, etc., a coal and lime depot etc.'

From this contemporary account it is clear that the station was not completed, by the opening day, but how much work was required to finish it is not clear. From the information given above it would appear that the passenger station was complete except for its overall roof and that the goods shed, in the station yard, had not been built. It is certain that within a short time of the opening the station consisted of two platforms, connected at the north end, with four tracks between them. Each track had a pair of turntables, one at each end of the platforms, with a connecting track between them so that engines or rolling stock could be released from the platform tracks onto the inner tracks.

At the opening the main station buildings must have been virtually complete

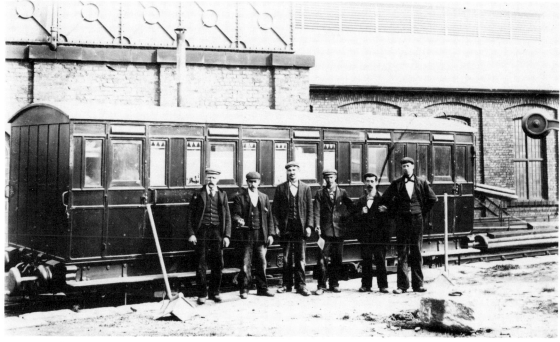

7. A group of workmen pose for a photograph in front of a North Eastern Railway coach which is standing adjacent to the old Engine House and the large brick-based water tank which was used to replenish the steam locomotives. On the extreme right is the counterbalance of a hand-operated crane – evidence that, by the time the photograph was taken, this site was in use as a goods depot.

Author's Collection.

Scarbro', York, Whitby, Pickering, Filey.							SUN.			
LEEDS	2 14	8 5	1255	3 10	5 0	..	Sat.	..	2 14	(a) Passengers for the Whitby Branch by trains marked (a) must change at Malton. These trains stop at Rillington only when passengers are booked for that place. (s) stop when required.—**Saturdays.**—Train from York at **3.30**, arr. at Scarbro' **5.35**.
	Gov	1&2	1&2	1&2	Gov		only.		Gov	
	mrn	mrn	aft	aft	aft				mrn	
YORK	6 0	9 45	3 0	4 30	7 0	..	3 30	..	6 0	
Haxby	6 11	9 56			7 11		3 41		6 11	
Strensall	6 18	10 3		4 44	7 18		3 48		6 18	
Flaxton	6 25	10 11	s	4 50	7 24		3 55		6 25	
Barton Hill	6 32	10 18	s	4 57	7 30		4 2		6 32	
Kirkham	6 41	10 28	..	5 6	7 39		4 11		6 41	
Castle Howard	6 44	10 31	..	s	7 42		4 14		6 44	
Hutton	6 50	10 37	..	..	7 48		4 20		6 50	
21¼ Malton	7 0	10 50	3 45	5 21	7 55		4 33		7 0	
Rillington, Whit	7 11	a	a	5 30	a		4 44		7 11	
Pickering arr	7 42	11 22	4 20	..	8 37		..		7 35	
Whitby .. arr.	9 0	12 40	5 40	..	9 55		..		9 0	
Knapton	7 18	11 5	..	s	8 18		4 51		7 18	
Heslerton	7 24	11 10	..	s	8 24		4 57		7 24	
Sherburn	7 33	11 19	s	s	8 31		5 6		7 33	
Ganton	7 39	11 24	s	5 46	8 39		5 12		7 39	
Seamer, Filey	7 49	11 34	4 20	5 57	9 49		5 22		7 49	
12¾ **SCARBRO'**	8 0	11 45	4 30	6 10	9 0		5 35		8 0	
Filey	8 10	11 58	4 55	..	..		..		3 40	
Bridlington	8 50	12 37	5 35	..	..		..		4 21	

							Thursdays only.			
Bridlington	..	8 0	..	..	2 5					
Filey	..	8 36	..	..	2 43					
	Gov	1&2	1&2	1&2	1,2,3	1,2,3		..	Gov	
	mrn	mrn	mrn	aft	Mail.				aft	
SCARBRO'	6 40	9 15	1010	1 55	6 45	3 10		..	6 45	
Seamer, Filey	6 47	9 23	..	2 2	6 52	3 17			6 52	
Ganton	6 55	9 33	s	2	7 0	3 25			7 0	
Sherburn	7 0	9 40	s		7 5	3 30			7 5	
Heslerton	7 8	9 47	s		7 13	3 35			7 13	
Knapton	7 13	9 50	s		7 18	3 40			7 18	
Rillington Whit	7 23	a		a	7 24	3 50			7 24	
Whitby .. dep.	..	8 10	..	1240	5 40				5 40	
Pickering dp.	6 30	9 30	..	2 5	7 0				7 0	
21 Malton	7 33	10 10	..	2 48	7 38	4 0			7 38	
Hutton	7 41		..	s	7 46				7 46	
Castle Howard	7 48	s	..	s	7 53				7 53	
Kirkham	7 51	10 23	..	s	7 56				7 56	
Barton Hill	8 1	10 31	..	3 6	8 6				8 6	
Flaxton	8 8	10 37	..	s	8 13				8 13	
Strensall	8 16		..	s	8 21				8 21	
Haxby	8 24		..	3 20	8 28				8 28	
42¾ **YORK**	8 40	11 5	1130	3 50	8 45				8 45	
LEEDS	11 9	1 0	1 0	5 10	10 49				10 57	

8. A page from *Ward's Railway Guide* of June 1865 showing the timetable for the York–Scarborough line only twenty years after it was opened. With fourteen intermediate stations the average time for the journey was two hours but the only express, with no stops and departing at 10-10 a.m., managed the journey in one hour and twenty minutes. There were four classes of fares – 1st, 2nd, 3rd and Government tickets which were the cheapest at rates laid down by Parliament.

Author's Collection.

9. The classic view of Scarborough station from an old postcard view taken when the forecourt, or station yard, was still surrounded by cast iron railings. On the extreme right is the dining and refreshment room – the kitchen and preparation rooms were in the cellar underneath together with a large brick-built oven. The sign on the entrance gate to the yard indicates that the Excursion platform could be reached by continuing on up Westborough, to the right. The clock was supplied by Potts of Leeds at a cost of £110 and was originally lit by gas which was paid for, together with the maintenance of the clock, by Scarborough Corporation.

Author's Collection.

and consisted of a large central booking office, to the left of which was the Superintendents Room, 2nd Class Waiting Room, Toilets, Porters Room and a Store Room. To the right of the booking office was the 1st Class Waiting Room, the Ladies Waiting Room and the Refreshment Rooms which stood at right angles to the main building. Above the Refreshment Room there was accommodation which was once the stationmaster's house but which was later used as the station hotel with ten bedrooms.

Considerable alterations and modifications have been made to the buildings and the layout of Scarborough station over the years and these make a fascinating study. There is not the space in a book of this size to describe them in detail but most of the major changes have been indicated in the text that follows or in the captions to the appropriate photographs.

10. This old postcard, which is postmarked 11 August 1908, shows the Royal Carriage passing the station on the occasion of the official opening of the Marine Drive, round the Castle Headland, by Princess Beatrice (H.R.H. Princess Henry of Battenburg)(see photograph 56). The photograph clearly shows the arched wall, and the original roof, of the cabstand adjacent to Westborough.

Author's Collection.

11. Scarborough station from the air in 1930. This shows the station at its most extensive development. Moving across the centre of the picture from left to right the following features are visible – the forecourt or station yard; the clock tower and carriage verandahs; the roof of the original station building; the double roof which covered the two original platforms and four tracks of 1845; the roof spanning across to the original goods shed, and its roof, both of which were extended at a later date, the difference between the old and new roofs can be seen. Beyond the roofs is the station goods yard, seen here occupied largely by a variety of coaching stock – illustrating the chronic problems of overcrowding at a seaside railway terminus. At the far side of the goods yard the long coal yard with its raised coal drops occupied the south-eastern extremity of the site.

Author's Collection.

INCREASING TRAFFIC

Mr F. W. Dowson, stationmaster at Scarborough from 1922 to 1943 (see page 36), saw traffic increase to quite remarkable proportions during his tenure here, especially during the 1930s, and the following is an annotated account, dated 2 February 1935, which he presented to the District Superintendent –

'Although the year 1933 shewed a substantial increase in passengers of approximately 133,000 arriving, as compared with 1932, it is still more gratifying to report that this figure was eclipsed last year which the following figures serve to shew –

	1934	1933
CENTRAL STATION	614,959	593,650
LONDSBRO RD STN	124,695	91,997
TOTAL	739,654	685,647

This gives an increase of 54,000 in tickets actually collected in 1934. In my report for 1933 I estimated that we had dealt with 85,000 passengers holding holiday season tickets over and above the figures given above. The tickets last year were definitely in excess of this figure; on 23 August the ticket collectors recorded the numbers of passengers who arrived holding these holiday season tickets and the figure at the close of the day was no less than 4379. On 6 September we repeated

12. (above left) A view of the station from about halfway along platform 1 showing the two gantries of N.E.R. slotted post signals which controlled access to and from the passenger station and goods yard (round the curve on the right). The station signal box appears in the centre of the picture.

Author's Collection.

13. (left) This photograph, taken in the 1980s, shows what was originally the first goods shed at the station – the building on the right. On the extreme left is the wall which marks the southernmost extent of the original passenger station of 1845. The roof in the centre, which spans the gap between the two buildings, was erected within two or three years of the opening to provide extra covered accommodation. Most of the goods traffic was moved to Gallows Close goods yard in stages during the 1890s up to 1903. As passenger traffic was increasing four new platforms were built – 6 and 7 underneath the roof in the centre of the photograph, platform 8 inside and 9 outside the old goods shed.

Ken Mills.

the arrangement when we registered 2308 season ticket holders. If, therefore, I include a figure of 125,000 for this type of traffic I do not feel I shall, in any wise, have exaggerated the extent of the traffic covering the whole of the period from 1st May to 31st October. This gives a gross total in round figures of inward passengers: 864,000 in 1934 as compared with 770,600 in 1933 and represents an increase last year of 94,000 passengers.

During the season the weekend traffic – both Saturdays and Sundays – taxed our resources severely and but for the relief provided by the new 1A platform for coast line trains, we should have been up against an almost insuperable task in relation to our maintaining anything approaching scheduled times at the peak period. The London traffic was again most satisfactory and neccessitated the duplication of the Scarborough Flier more frequently than any previous year, partly due to increased traffic and in a measure to the load being definitely limited to thirteen bogies of the vestibuled type.

Sunday Excursions: The traffic continues to grow and the numbers of evening and observation excursions run to Scarborough proved very popular indeed. The demand upon the Central station platforms for ordinary trains on Sundays was such that from the 5th August to the 9th September, inclusive, the Londesborough Road station was open to augment the facilities for dealing with the excursion traffic. On these six Sundays we dealt with forty-three trains off which we collected 13,726 tickets. During the period, June to September inclusive, Sunday excursion trains to the Central station were 275 off which we collected 91,875 excursion tickets; this does not take into account ordinary passengers or weekly season ticket holders who made use of excursion trains.

A total of 124,471 platform tickets were issued during 1934 which brought in receipts of just over £518.' (This figure may sound small by today's standards but it was enough to pay the stationmaster's salary for the whole year!).

14 & 15. (right) Crowded scenes at Scarborough station with the famous locomotive, *Flying Scotsman* on the Kings Cross – Scarborough express 'The Scarborough Flier'. The London & North Eastern Railway introduced this through summer express in 1923 when it took four and a half hours. By 1935 the time had been cut to 3 hours 55 minutes for the 230 mile journey. The service was suspended in 1939 but was reintroduced on 5 June 1950, departing from Scarborough at 11-30 a.m.

Scarborough Evening News.

16. North Eastern Railway '1463' class locomotive, number 1468, on a train of mixed passenger rolling stock, passing Falsgrave signal box (see photograph 33). It was the practice, before Scarborough became a closed station with ticket barriers in 1913, to collect passengers' tickets before the trains entered the station. The boards between the tracks in the foreground allowed the ticket collectors to move from coach to coach in the days of non-corridor coaches. Whilst the coaches stood here the engines ran round their trains in order to propel them into the station before this practice was banned due to the number of accidents.

Author's Collection.

17. The driver of this B1 class engine, 61289, hands the single line pouch and tablet to the signalman at Falsgrave after emerging from the tunnel. Falsgrave tunnel was built in the early 1880s to allow the Scarborough & Whitby Railway to connect with the North Eastern Railway, when it was opened in 1885.

Ken Hoole.

18. British Railways class A8, 69867, hauls a train from Whitby into Scarborough, having just emerged from Falsgrave tunnel, on 5 July 1952.

Ken Hoole.

19. This British Railways mixed traffic locomotive, 77013 a Scarborough based engine, hauls in an excursion train having just emerged from Falsgrave tunnel behind platform 1A where a crowd of passengers await the train for Whitby and Middlesbrough on 14 August 1954.

Ken Hoole.

20. Former LMS 'Royal Scot' class, 46115 *Scots Guardsman*, leaving Scarborough on a return Castleford excursion on 2 June 1963. The engine's home shed was Manchester, Longsight.

Fred Rowntree.

21. Class B1, 61385, propels a Route Instruction Car into 1A platform on 15 April 1961. These vehicles were used as mobile schools for drivers learning a new route. The large windows, at the sides and ends, enabled all those under instruction to have a good view of tracks and signals. The seats were also tiered up from the ends to the centre of the vehicle which was normally propelled by an engine coupled at the rear.

Fred Rowntree.

22. In order to accommodate excursion traffic at the station the platforms now known as 1 & 2 were added in 1883 and separate waiting rooms and other facilities provided in this building adjacent to platform 1. The building, later used as the parcels office, can be seen on this photograph taken in 1896. There was a ticket office on the extreme right and the signs next to the doors indicate that there was, from right to left – a 'General Waiting Room', 'Ladies Room', 'Gentlemen', and, in the far corner, the 'Way Out' which led up through a long passage onto Westborough so that access for day trippers and excursionists was independent of the main station.

Author's Collection.

NEW EXCURSION STATION

When the excursion platforms, 1 and 2, at the station, were found to be inadequate for the increasing traffic, in the late 1890s, the N.E.R. Company obtained powers by Act of Parliament to build a completely new station for the excursion trains. The site eventually chosen was that of the old Engine House yard and the cost of the new building was almost £7,500. A new bridge to replace the Washbeck viaduct (the 'Five Arches'), to accommodate the extra tracks, cost nearly £5,500, the four miles of carriage sidings, at Northstead, just over £4,000, and a new 'Washbeck' signal box cost almost £400.

The new station was opened on 8 June 1908 and consisted of one through platform almost 300 yards in length and a shorter bay platform just over 250 yards long. Most excursion trains arrived at the through platform, disgorged their happy throngs, and then went forward through Falsgrave tunnel and up to the carriage sidings where the trains were stored for the day and the engines turned, coaled and watered ready for the return workings in the evening.

The circulating and waiting area at the station was well organised as rows of barriers were set up so that passengers could be segregated into groups according to which train they were returning on. This enabled the staff to ensure that most passengers caught the right train despite the fact that many trains departed within minutes of each other. Some passengers had the opinion that Londesborough Road station was more like a cattle market but the system worked well.

The excursion station did occasionally handle ordinary traffic, particularly when there was a derailment, or track relaying at the Central station. An early morning train from Middlesbrough used to stop here, to allow school pupils to get off, during term time in the 1950s.

A member of staff recalled that Lloyd George, the famous politician, once gave a speech on the platform here and Londesborough Road station has been used for a variety of purposes over the years – in World War One as a parade ground for troops, in 1920 to store Robinson's coaches (see photograph 48), in the 1930s as a wet weather rehearsal area for the Open Air Theatre performers, and as an Army supply depot in World War Two. Decreasing traffic led to the closure of the station on 4 July 1966 although the last train had departed on 24 August 1963.

23. An old postcard view which shows Londesborough Road excursion station shortly after it was opened in 1908. Its position, nearly half a mile further from the seafront, by road, than the Central station, made it unpopular with holidaymakers returning to their trains after a hectic and tiring day on the beach.

Author's Collection.

24. (right) The vast expanse of Londesborough Road excursion station is well-illustrated on this old postcard which shows that there were about eighteen members of staff based here at one time.

Author's Collection.

25. This remarkable photograph, from an old postcard, came to light only a few days before this book had to be with the publishers! It shows N.E.R. class '398' number 116, with a train at platform 1, Londesborough Road station, being admired by a crowd of smartly-dressed onlookers. On the back of the card is written – '1st Excursion train to arrive at the New Station, Scarborough'. This would therefore appear to be the inaugural train of 8 June 1908 and the top-hatted gentleman (left) may be the Scarborough stationmaster Mr G. Brown.

Author's Collection.

26. Bertram Mills Circus, a regular visitor to Scarborough in the 1950s, detrains onto number 2 platform at Londesborough Road station ably assisted by station staff Tommy Goudry and Tommy Pool.

Jack Layton Collection.

27. Scarborough's first L.M.S. tank engine, 42084, on the 11-40 a.m. to Middlesbrough on 5 April 1952, near Londesborough Road station.

Ken Hoole.

28. The first Diesel Multiple Unit, in Scarborough, stands at platform 1, Londesborough Road station on 3 November 1955 on the occasion of a test run from York with a party of officials.

Ken Hoole.

29. A mixed goods train, with B.R. standard locomotive 77000 in charge, runs alongside Londesborough Road station having just emerged from Falsgrave tunnel after departing from Gallows Close goods yard on 29 May 1960.

Norman Skinner.

30. The North Eastern locomotive yard, outside the straight shed near Seamer Road, in about 1912. The engines are, right to left – class 'O' tank 540, class 'C1' 1805 and a class 'Q' with its distinctive clerestory-roofed cab. Number 1902, of this class, was shedded here in 1920. *W. Leslie Good.*

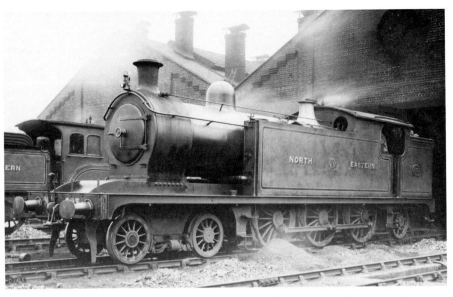

31. North Eastern Railway class 'W' (L.N.E.R. A6) 693 stands outside the straight shed in about 1920. This class of engine was built especially for hauling passenger trains on the steep and winding coast line from Scarborough to Saltburn.

Author's Collection.

32. North Eastern class 'J' 1579 outside the straight shed. These engines had a single pair of driving wheels measuring 7.5 feet (nearly 2 metres) in diameter. They were used for a number of years on the Leeds – Scarborough services around the turn of the century. *W. Leslie Good.*

33. L.N.E.R. class 'E5', 1468, originally N.E.R. '1463' or 'Tennant' class, inside the roundhouse. They were also employed on the Leeds – Scarborough service and were noted for keeping very good time and for negotiating the curves at Kirkham Abbey very smoothly. *Author's Collection.*

THE ENGINE SHEDS

The first engine shed at Scarborough was the one on the site of what was later Londesborough Road station and which is illustrated in photographs 6 and 7. By 1880 the engine accommodation was found to be insufficient and the N.E.R. Company drew up plans for a roundhouse to hold 13 engines on a new site next to Seamer Road, near Seamer Street. The building, which contrary to its name was square, contained a turntable, 44 feet 8 inches in diameter in the centre, with short 'roads' radiating off it to stable the engines. The cost of the building was about £4,500 and the turntable £335 and this facility was completed by the end of 1881.

Within seven years of the completion of the roundhouse the engine accommodation was again found to be inadequate and plans were drawn up for a new straight shed to house 24 engines on eight parallel tracks. The building cost nearly £10,000 but the 50 ft turntable cost only £305 and this was installed in front of the roundhouse. The new shed was in use by 1890 and, together with the old roundhouse, provided covered accommodation for 37 engines at Scarborough.

In later years the roundhouse was used to store locomotives which required repairs or had been withdrawn from service, especially during the winter months when fewer engines were needed. The straight shed suffered from land subsidence in the 1950s and large wooden buttresses were used to support the east end of the building and in 1959 the southern half of the building was demolished.

With the change-over from steam to diesel traction in the 1960s the steam depot was closed, on 20 May 1963, although visiting steam locomotives continued to use the yard until 1967. The remaining half of the straight shed was demolished in 1966 but the earlier roundhouse survived until June 1971.

34. An aerial view of the locomotive yard alongside Seamer Road. The locomotive straight shed is on the upper left of the photograph and the large complex of Scarborough Gasworks is clearly visible on the right. The roundhouse shed is just off the top of the photograph, together with the large turntable. Gasworks signal box can be seen in the centre between the locomotive yard and the main lines. An interesting diversion was caused on 21 October 1936 when a coal wagon was pushed through the end of the Gas Company's shed, by a little over-enthusiastic shunting, and landed in the yard below. The York breakdown crane had to be sent to retrieve its remains six days later.

Author's Collection.

35. Engine 1269 standing in the locomotive yard. Originally the engine had been built as a 4-4-0 for the Stockton & Darlington Railway in 1874 when it was known as a 'Ginx's Baby'. Author's Collection.

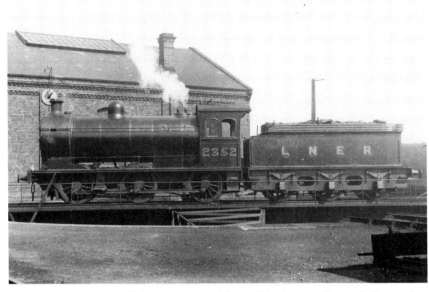

36. L.N.E.R. class J27, 2352, on the turntable outside the roundhouse in September 1938. These engines were mainly used for the goods and mineral traffic. Fred Rowntree Collection.

37. Another class W, 686, together with a Sentinel Steam Railcar, *British Queen*, at the south end of the locomotive yard in 1932. The steam railcars, introduced in 1928, were used on the branch lines in the area, particularly during the winter months when traffic was light. T. E. Rounthwaite.

38. A popular class of engine, in this area, was the D49 the members of which were all named after shires and foxhunts. This is 62765, *The Goathland*, on the turntable. The nameplate, with its cast brass running fox, can be seen above the front driving wheel. Fred Rowntree.

39. Another D49, 62723, *Nottinghamshire* on the turntable on 13 August 1960. This was one of the last four members of this class to be withdrawn from the North Eastern Region in 1961.

Fred Rowntree.

40. Two former L.M.S. class 5 engines, 45449 and 44951, stand in the remains of the southern half of the straight shed on 26 May 1966. In the background are the massive buildings of the former Scarborough Gasworks.

Fred Rowntree.

41. The first visit of a British Railways 'Britannia' class locomotive to Scarborough, 70053 *Moray Firth*, which proves to be a very tight fit on the turntable on 10 December 1958.

Fred Rowntree.

42. British Railways, former L.N.E.R., class A2/3, 60515 *Sun Stream* in store, in the straight shed in 1962, minus its nameplates which had been removed for safe-keeping.

Norman Skinner.

43. An unusual visitor to Scarborough – ex-Seaham Harbour (*Earl of Londonderry*) railway engine number 9. The building in the background is the distinctive Westborough Methodist Chapel.

Author's Collection.

44. N.E.R. 'Bogie Tank Passenger' engine, 954, at Scarborough station. This engine was built in 1874. In later years, as trains grew heavier, the class was allocated to small goods and shunting duties.

Author's Collection.

45. Two ex-L.N.E.R. J94 engines were stationed here between about 1946 and 1950. Some were later sent here for storage and one of them, 8061, is seen here leaving Scarborough under its own steam on 18 October 1962.

Fred Rowntree.

46. British Railways standard class 3 tank engine, 82029, was one of the last steam locomotives to be stationed at Scarborough and was photographed in the locomotive yard on 4 September 1960.

Fred Rowntree.

CHAR-A-BANCS

The popular char-a-banc trips, at Scarborough, were introduced by the N.E.R. Company in April 1906. The service ran from the station forecourt and by 1914 there were twelve different tours which departed at 10-15 a.m. and 2-15 p.m., returning by 1-00 p.m. and 6.00 p.m. respectively, for half-day tours. Four of the tours were full day excursions, the longest of which, to Rievaulx and Helmsley, . involved a round trip of 73 miles at a cost of 7/6d (38p).

Most of the vehicles, which were on Durkopp, Fiat and Saurer chassis, had six rows of seats rising in three tiers towards the back. In addition to the driver there was a guard, or assistant motorman, and the maximum permitted speed of the vehicles was 12 miles per hour. Portable ladders were used for access to the rear seats and the char-a-bancs carried up to 33 passengers.

The shortest tour from Scarborough station forecourt was to Scalby and Burniston, a round trip of seven miles, for which the fare was 1/- (5p). The more adventurous could go to Scalby, Hackness and Forge Valley, a round trip of 18 miles, morning or afternoon, for 2/6d (13p). A trip to Cayton Bay, Filey and Seamer, 20 miles, also cost 2/6d. Tickets were issued at the motor car office in the station forecourt and, whilst no reduction was made for children individually, two children under 13 years old, would be conveyed on one ticket.

47. (above right) Two North Eastern Railway char-a-bancs in the station forecourt prior to setting off on their trips to Forge Valley and Filey. By the time they returned the photographer had developed and printed his negatives and was able to sell copies to the passengers.

Colin Spink Collection.

48. (right) After World War One the motor tours were operated by Robinson's and this photograph shows three of their fleet of torpedo-bodied vehicles (two Leyland and a Daimler) in the station forecourt in about 1920. The motor tour booking office can be seen on the left.

Colin Spink Collection.

49. (centre pages, overleaf) *The Scarborough Summer Timetable* for 1961 when all ten platforms at the Central station were in use as well as the two at Londesborough Road station. At this time the coast line to Whitby and Middlesbrough was still in use and there was also a service to Filey Holiday Camp station. The many long distance Saturday only trains went to Edinburgh, Glasgow, Manchester, Newcastle, Bradford, Derby, Birmingham, Sheffield, Leicester, Swindon and Bristol. 'The Scarborough Flier' was still operating on Saturdays and also on Sundays at the height of the season.

Author's Collection.

BRITISH RAILWAYS

DEPARTURE OF TRAINS

FROM

SCARBOROUGH

12th JUNE TO 10th SEPTEMBER INCLUSIVE 1961

THE TELEPHONE NUMBER OF SCARBOROUGH ENQUIRY OFFICE IS 3486

WEEKDAYS

HOUR	TO	PLATFORM
am 6 45	Saturdays only not after 26th August, Filey, Filey Holiday Camp	5
7 15	Seamer, Malton, York; Darlington, Newcastle; Doncaster, Leeds (City), Huddersfield, Stalybridge, Manchester (Exchange)	3
7 23	Hull and intermediate stations except Carnaby, and Arram	1
8 2	Malton, York, Darlington, Newcastle. Edinburgh (Waverley), Glasgow (Queen Street); Sheffield (Midland), Derby (Midland), Birmingham (New Street); Doncaster, London (King's Cross); Sheffield (Vic.), Nottingham (Vic.), Leicester (Central), Oxford, Reading, Southampton, Bournemouth (West), Church Fenton, Leeds (City), Huddersfield, Stalybridge, Manchester (Exchange), Liverpool (Lime Street)	2
8 10	Saturdays 15th July to 19th August inclusive Darlington, Durham, Newcastle, Edinburgh (Wav.)	2
8 15	Filey, Bridlington, Driffield, Hull	6
8 28	Hull and intermediate stations except Speeton	1
8 35	Saturdays only, 15th July to 12th August Northallerton, Darlington, Durham, Newcastle, Morpeth, Alnmouth, Berwick, Edinburgh, Polmont, Falkirk (High), Glasgow (Queen St.)	1
9 20	Saturdays only Leeds (City), Huddersfield, Manchester (Victoria)	3
9 25	Middlesbrough and intermediate stations	{7SX / 1ASO} 4
9 55	Saturdays only York, Micklefield, Garforth, Cross Gates, Leeds (City), Huddersfield, Stalybridge, Manchester (Exchange), Liverpool (Lime Street)	3
10 5	Saturdays only Seamer, Malton, York, Darlington, Newcastle, Sheffield (Mid.), Derby (Mid.), Birmingham (New Street), Doncaster, Leeds (City), Huddersfield, Manchester (Exchange)	3
10 10	Saturdays excepted Seamer, Malton, York, Darlington, Newcastle, Sheffield (Mid.), Doncaster; Leeds (City), Huddersfield, Manchester (Exchange); Liverpool (Lime Street); through portion for London (King's Cross) (RESTAURANT CAR from York)	3
10 15	Middlesbrough and intermediate stations except Commondale and Kildale	{5SX / 1ASO} 8/9
10 25	Saturdays only, not after 2nd September Dunbar, Edinburgh (Waverley); Falkirk (High), Glasgow (Queen Street)	2
10 42	Saturdays only Grantham, London (King's Cross) (THE SCARBOROUGH FLYER—RESTAURANT CAR)	2
10 45	Saturdays excepted Filey, Flamborough, Bridlington	6
10 50	Saturdays only, Commences 24th June Stockton, West Hartlepool, Seaham, Sunderland, Newcastle (via Gilling)	4
11 5	Saturdays excepted Malton, York, Darlington, Newcastle, Sheffield (Mid.)	2
11 5	Saturdays only York, Leeds (City), Shipley Bradford (Forster Square), Huddersfield, Manchester (Exchange), Liverpool (Lime Street)	1
11 10	Saturdays only, 8th July to 2nd September inclusive, Filey, Filey Holiday Camp	6
11 20	Saturdays only, not after 26th August York, Leeds (City), Huddersfield, Normanton, Wakefield (Kirkgate), Todmorden, Rochdale, Manchester (Victoria)	1
11 25	Saturdays only Filey, Bridlington, Driffield, Beverley, Hull	7
11 30	Saturdays excepted Hull and intermediate stations except Speeton and Carnaby	5
11 31	Middlesbrough and intermediate stations	{7SX / 1ASO} 4
11 32	Saturdays only 8th July to 26th August Chesterfield (Mid.), Belper, Derby (Mid.)	4
11 37	Saturdays only Bridlington and intermediate stations (except Speeton), Driffield, Beverley, Cottingham, Hull	

WEEKDAYS—continued

HOUR	TO	PLATFORM
pm 5 30	8th July to 2nd September inclusive, also Saturday 9th September, York, Selby, Doncaster, Rotherham (Cen.), Sheffield (Vic.), Nottingham (Vic.), Loughborough, Leicester (Cen.), Rugby (Cen.), Banbury, Swindon	4
5 47	Cloughton, Staintondale, Ravenscar, Robin Hood's Bay, Whitby (Town), Grosmont, Glaisdale, Danby, Castleton, Battersby, Great Ayton, Nunthorpe, Ormesby, Middlesbrough, (extended to Thornaby, Stockton, Billingham, West Hartlepool on Saturdays also Mondays to Fridays 24th July to 25th August inclusive)	{7SX / 1ASO}
6 0	Saturdays only Filey, Bridlington and intermediate stations to Hull (except Carnaby)	5
6 0	Saturdays excepted Seamer, Filey, Bridlington and intermediate stations to Hull (except Carnaby)	5
6 20	Malton, York, Sheffield (Mid.), Darlington, Newcastle, Church Fenton, Garforth, Cross Gates, Leeds (City), Huddersfield, Stalybridge, Manchester (Exchange), Liverpool (Lime Street)	2
6 22	Saturdays only, also Mondays to Fridays 24th July to 25th August inclusive, Cloughton, Staintondale, Ravenscar, Robin Hood's Bay, Whitby (Town), Grosmont, Glaisdale, Castleton, Battersby, Nunthorpe, Ormesby, Middlesbrough	7
6 30	Saturdays only Malton, York, Darlington, Durham, Newcastle, (1st July to 2nd September through train Selby, Doncaster)	3
6 45	Saturdays excepted 17th July to 1st September Malton, York (17th July to 18th August through train to Church Fenton, Micklefield, Garforth, Cross Gates, Leeds)	3
6 52	Middlesbrough and intermediate stations (except Fyling Hall, Hawsker, Great Ayton.) Thornaby, Eaglescliffe, Dinsdale, Darlington	6
7 15	Bridlington and intermediate stations (except Speeton), Nafferton, Driffield, Beverley, Cottingham, Hull	5
7 20	Saturdays excepted 10th July to 18th August York, Cross Gates, Leeds, Huddersfield	1
7 28	Cloughton, Staintondale, Ravenscar, Robin Hood's Bay, Whitby (Town), Grosmont, Glaisdale, Castleton, Battersby, Middlesbrough, Thornaby, Eaglescliffe, Dinsdale, Darlington	7
7 30	York, Wakefield (Kirkgate) and intermediate stations	3
7 50	Micklefield, Garforth, Cross Gates, Leeds (City)	2
7 52	Saturdays only, also Mondays to Fridays 24th July to 25th August inclusive, Cloughton, Staintondale, Ravenscar, Robin Hood's Bay, Whitby (Town), Grosmont, Glaisdale, Danby, Castleton, Battersby, Nunthorpe, Ormesby, Middlesbrough	9
8 0	Malton, York, Darlington, Newcastle, Edinburgh (Waverley), Glasgow (Queen Street); Sheffield (Mid.), Derby (Mid.), Birmingham (New Street); Nottingham (Victoria), Leicester (Central); Doncaster, London (King's Cross); Huddersfield, Stalybridge, Manchester (Exchange)	1
8 20	Middlesbrough and intermediate stations except Commondale and Kildale	8
8 25	Seamer, Filey, Hunmanby, Bempton, Flamborough, Bridlington, Nafferton, Driffield, Hull and intermediate stations	5
9 15	17th July to 2nd September, Malton, York, Pontefract (Baghill), Sheffield (Mid.), Leeds (City); Darlington, Newcastle, Edinburgh, Glasgow	1

Main Departures

HOUR	TO	PLATFORM
10 10	Leeds (City), Huddersfield, Stalybridge, Manchester (Vic. and Exchange)	3
10 28	Malton, York, Darlington, Newcastle, Edinburgh (Waverley); Sheffield (New Street); Doncaster, London (King's Cross), Leeds (City), Huddersfield, Stalybridge, Manchester (Victoria and Exchange)	5
10 35	Hull and intermediate stations except Carnaby	3
10 40	Commencing 16th July Malton, York, Grantham, London (King's Cross), (THE SCARBOROUGH FLYER — RESTAURANT CAR); change York for Leeds (City); Manchester (Exchange), Liverpool (Lime Street); Darlington, Newcastle, Edinburgh (Waverley); Sheffield (Midland), Derby (Midland), Birmingham (New Street), Bristol (Temple Meads), Doncaster	1A
11 35	Whitby and intermediate stations except Fyling Hall and Hawsker	5
pm 2 30	9th July to 13th August Bridlington and intermediate stations (except Seamer)	3
2 35	Malton, York, Darlington, Newcastle, Edinburgh (Waverley), Glasgow (Queen Street); London (King's Cross), Sheffield (Mid), Derby (Mid), Birmingham (New Street); Leeds (City), Huddersfield, Stalybridge, Church Fenton, Leeds (City), Ulleskelf, Manchester (Exchange), Liverpool (Lime Street)	1A
5 0	Whitby and intermediate stations except Fyling Hall and Hawsker	1A
5 20	Until 27th August Cloughton, Staintondale, Ravenscar, Robin Hood's Bay, Whitby (Town), Grosmont, Glaisdale, Castleton, Battersby, Ormesby, Middlesbrough, York, Harrogate, Micklefield, Garforth, Cross Gates, Leeds (City), Huddersfield, Stalybridge, Manchester (Exchange), Liverpool (Lime Street)	3
5 30	Middlesbrough and intermediate stations (except Fyling Hall, Hawsker, Egton, Lealholm, Danby, Commondale, Kildale, Great Ayton, Nunthorpe, Thornaby, Stockton	1A
5 47	Middlesbrough and intermediate stations (except Hayburn Wyke, Fyling Hall, Hawsker, Ruswarp, Sleights)	1A
5 55	2nd July to 3rd, September Malton, York, Darlington, Newcastle	1A
6 15	Hull and intermediate stations except Carnaby	2
6 30	Robin Hood's Bay, Whitby (Town), Grosmont, Glaisdale, Castleton, Battersby, Middlesbrough, Thornaby, Eaglescliffe, Dinsdale, Darlington	5 / 1A
6 58	Leeds (Exchange), Huddersfield, Stalybridge, Manchester (Exchange), Liverpool (Lime St.)	2
7 0	Cloughton, Staintondale, Ravenscar, Robin Hood's Bay, Whitby (Town), Grosmont, Glaisdale, Castleton, Battersby, Great Ayton, Nunthorpe, Ormesby, Middlesbrough, Thornaby, Stockton, Billingham, West Hartlepool	1A
7 10	9th July to 3rd September Malton, York, Darlington, Newcastle, Sheffield	4
7 30	Malton, York, Derby (Mid.), Birmingham (New Street)	3
8 0	Middlesbrough and intermediate stations (except Fyling Hall and Hawsker)	6
8 20	Micklefield, Garforth, Cross Gates, Leeds (City), Huddersfield, Shipley, Bradford (Forster Square)	1
8 30	Malton, York, Darlington, Newcastle, Edinburgh (Waverley); Doncaster, London (King's Cross); Huddersfield, Manchester (Exchange), Basford	3
8 40	Seamer, Filey, Bridlington, Driffield, Beverley, Hull	5
12 30	Tamworth (H.L.), Birmingham (New Street), King's Norton	4
12 50	Saturdays only Seamer, Malton, York; and intermediate stations to Leeds (City), Huddersfield, Stalybridge, Manchester (Victoria), Liverpool (Exchange), Darlington, Newcastle, Edinburgh (Waverley), Glasgow (Queen Street); London (King's Cross)	5
12 50	Hull and intermediate stations except Speeton & Burton Agnes (calls Speeton on Saturdays only)	8
1 0	24th July to 26th August Whitby Town and intermediate stations	9
1 20	Saturdays only 15th July to 19th August incl. Edinburgh (Wav.), Falkirk (H.), Glasgow (Q. St.)	3
1 20	Saturdays only York, Darlington, Newcastle, Edinburgh (Wav.), Glasgow (Queen St.), London (King's Cross), Sheffield (Mid.), Derby (Mid.), Birmingham (New St.), Leeds (City)	3
2 0	Saturdays excepted, Malton, York, Darlington, Newcastle, Edinburgh (Wav.), Glasgow (Queen Street); Sheffield (Mid.), Derby (Mid.), Birmingham (New Street); Peterborough, London (King's Cross), Leeds (City), Huddersfield, Stalybridge, Manchester (Exchange), Liverpool (Lime Street)	2
2 5	Saturdays only, commences 24th June Moorthorpe, Bolton-on-Dearne, Rotherham (Cen.), Sheffield (Victoria)	
2 10	Saturdays only, also Mondays to Fridays 24th July to 25th August inclusive, Whitby and intermediate stations	6SX 1ASO
2 10	Saturdays only, 15th July to 26th August York, Grantham, London (King's Cross)	1
2 17	Malton, York, Church Fenton, Leeds (City), Huddersfield, Stalybridge, Manchester (Exchange), Liverpool (Lime Street)	3
2 25	Saturdays only 8th July to 2nd September, Filey, Filey Holiday Camp	6
2 30	Saturdays only, not after 2nd September York, Pontefract (Baghill), Moorthorpe, Bolton-on-Dearne, Swinton (Town), Parkgate and Rawmarsh, Rotherham (Masboro), Sheffield (Midland), Chesterfield (Mid.), Belper, Derby, Burton-on-Trent, Tamworth, Wilnecote, Castle Bromwich, Barnt Green, Gloucester (Eastgate), Mangotsfield, Bristol (Temple-Meads)	2
2 42	Cloughton, Staintondale, Ravenscar, Robin Hood's Bay, Whitby (Town)	7SX 1ASO 5
2 55	Hull and intermediate stations except Speeton, Flamborough and Carnaby	2
3 10	Seamer, Malton, York, Darlington, Newcastle, Sheffield (Midland), Leeds (City), Huddersfield, Manchester (Exchange)	4
3 50	Saturdays only, 1st July to 2nd September York, Darlington, Newcastle, Leeds (City), Huddersfield, Manchester (Exchange), Liverpool (Lime Street)	3
4 5	Seamer, Malton, York, Newcastle, Sheffield (Mid), Derby (Mid), Birmingham (New Street); London (King's Cross); Manchester (Vic), Liverpool (Ex.), Leeds (City), Huddersfield, Manchester (Ex.), Liverpool (Lime Street)	
4 25	Middlesbrough and intermediate stations	6SX 1ASO 2
4 30	Hull and intermediate stations except Speeton	3
5 15	Seamer, Malton, York, London (King's Cross), Harrogate, Church Fenton, Leeds (City), Huddersfield Stalybridge, Manchester (Exchange), Liverpool (Lime Street) and intermediate stations to Bradford (Forster Square)	

Through carriages to stations shown in bold type

The train services and platforming arrangements shown here are subject to alteration or cancellation at short notice and do not necessarily apply at Bank and Public Holiday periods

LONDESBOROUGH ROAD (SATURDAYS ONLY)

HOUR	TO	PLATFORM	HOUR	TO	PLATFORM
am 9 40	29th July to 26th August Chesterfield (Mid.), Alfreton, Pye Bridge, Codnor Park and Ironville, Langley Mill, Ilkeston Junction, Trowell, Stapleford & Sandiacre, Long Eaton, Trent, Loughborough, Syston, Leicester (London Road)	2	am 11 50	Filey, Bridlington, Kirkby Bentinck, Hucknall (Central), Bulwell Common, Nottingham (Vic), Arkwright Street, Loughborough (Cen), Leicester (Cen).	1
pm 10 0	8th July to 2nd September Filey, Bridlington, Pontefract, Barnsley (Ex.), Penistone, Guide Bridge, Manchester (Piccadilly)	1	pm 2 35	15th July to 26th August Filey, Bridlington, Doncaster, Retford, Ollerton, Edwinstowe, Mansfield, Sutton-in-Ashfield, Kirkby-in-Ashfield, Hucknall (Cen.), Bulwell Common, Basford (North)	2
11 15	24th June to 26th August Filey, Bridlington, Thornhill, Mirfield, Brighouse, Sowerby Bridge, Hebden Bridge, Todmorden, Littleborough, Rochdale, Bury, Bolton, Wigan, Liverpool (Ex Forster Square)	2			

Through carriages and platforming arrangements shown here are subject to alteration or cancellation at short notice and do not necessarily apply at Bank and Public Holiday periods

No. 21   Published by British Railways (N.E. Region) 5/61 B.R. 35121/66   Printed in Great Britain   (R21103)Herald York—B6)

IT'S QUICKER BY RAIL   THE SCARBOROUGH FLIER

1D a mile MONTHLY RETURN TICKETS

are issued to

SCARBOROUGH
from ANYWHERE

Available by ANY TRAIN on ANY DAY and the

Outward and Return journeys may be completed on any day within a calendar month of the date of issue—you can break your journey when, where, and as often as you like on the direct route.

FIRST CLASS 1½d. a mile

Children up to 14 years half-fare.

● including the Scarborough Flier or other fast Restaurant Car Expresses.

PASSENGER TRAINS

Over the years there has been a tremendous variety of passenger traffic into Scarborough station. There were regular services southwards to Filey, Bridlington and Hull; westward to Malton, York, Leeds and Pickering; and northward to Whitby, Saltburn and Middlesbrough. For the railway enthusiast, and the holidaymaker the most interesting were the excursion trains which came from most parts of the country. This traffic was hauled, over the years, by a great variety of 'foreign' engines and this made the railway scene at Scarborough such an interesting one.

50. The cover of a leaflet giving details of cheap tourist fares to Scarborough and illustrating the town's most famous train, 'The Scarborough Flier' (see caption 14/15). The prices of 1935 are of interest as the fares to Scarborough were, from Aberdeen £3.46, Birmingham £1.55, Bradford 75p, Plymouth £3.57, Sheffield 87p and London Kings Cross £2.16.

Author's Collection.

51. From the sublime to the ridiculous – class G5, 67273, pushes its diminutive train, one of the smallest locomotive-worked passenger services out of Scarborough, to Pickering on 9 July 1949 having departed at 6-40 p.m. The Seamer – Pickering branch, which opened in May 1882, closed in June 1950.

Fred Rowntree Collection.

Before the 'Grouping' in 1923 trains and engines from many of the old companies could be seen here, including Great Northern, Great Central, Midland, Lancashire & Yorkshire and the Great Eastern. The rolling stock, from the same companies, varied from short four-wheeled sparsely upholstered coaches, which provided a very uncomfortable ride as they clattered and shook along the track, to the splendidly upholstered and luxuriously comfortable long, bogie-wheeled, corridor coaches.

52. Two class V2 locomotives double-head an excursion train into Scarborough past Washbeck signal box and its fine gantry of N.E.R. slotted-post, lower quadrant, signals.
R. A. Hodges.

53. A3 locomotive, 60084 *Trigo*, hauls the 09-20 to Manchester out of Scarborough station on 27 July 1963.

David Bointon.

54. The old and the new order at Scarborough station on 3 September 1966 – steam on the works trip from Halifax at platform 2, diesel haulage on the train at platform 1.
Ken Hoole.

55. The Scarborough Touring Van – advertising with a difference which could truly be described as 'putting the show on the road'. This smart vehicle, with an Albion chassis, deep blue bodywork, fawn wheels and lettering in gold, was augmented in London when Sir Ralph Wedgwood (Chairman of the L.N.E.R.) and the Mayor of Scarborough, in the presence of representatives of the L.N.E.R., the Scarborough Corporation and the press, together unveiled the new Scarborough Touring Van. The three 'pictures' (there were two on the 'off' side) were actually three-dimensional dioramas of the South Bay, North Bay and Peasholm. The van was filled with tourist literature which was handed out by the staff. After touring round London, where it was a great success, the van set off to tour round England and Southern Scotland.

Author's Collection.

56. An unusual view of platform 3 at Scarborough station decorated for the arrival of Royalty. Princess Beatrice (H.R.H. Princess Henry of Battenburg) came to officially open the Marine Drive in August 1908.

Author's Collection.

57. Her Majesty Queen Elizabeth II and H.R.H. Prince Phillip arriving at Scarborough station on 2 July 1975. They were met by the Lord Lieutenant of the North Riding of Yorkshire, Sir William Worsley.

Jack Layton Collection.

58. Prime Minister Harold Macmillan and Mr R. A. Butler walk down the platform on the occasion of a Conservative Party Conference in 1960.

Jack Layton Collection.

59. Labour Prime Minister, Harold Wilson, complete with Gannex coat and pipe, hands in his ticket at the barrier closely watched by T. T. Wardell who makes sure!

Jack Layton Collection.

60. (top left) Gallows Close goods yard looking south from Wykeham Street bridge in 1981, shortly before closure. On the extreme left is the curved mouth of Falsgrave tunnel whilst the brick building towards the right of the photograph is the original North Eastern Railway goods station and warehouse opened in 1902.

Ken Mills.

61. (above) A copy of the notice announcing the opening of increased facilities at Gallows Close on 13 June 1899. In 1956 a retiring member of the goods staff recalled that in the past they had dealt with up to 100 wagons of fresh fish, including herring and kippers, daily from Gallows Close.

Author's Collection.

62. (left) A view from the other side of Wykeham Street bridge showing the smaller, northern section of Gallows Close goods yard. In the centre is Gallows Close signal box (see photograph 80) and beyond that, to the left, Hibernia Street bridge.

Alan King.

THE GOODS DEPARTMENT

Goods and mineral traffic has been dealt with at various locations in Scarborough over the years. At first it was handled at the station yard and later at the old Engine House yard and Falsgrave sidings. The most important site, however, was undoubtedly Gallows Close goods yard which the N.E.R. Company started to use in about 1894. It became the main goods station in 1899 and the large goods warehouse and transship station were opened in 1902 when the company completed the expansion of the facilities here. Rail access to and from Gallows Close was through the single line Falsgrave tunnel, which was completed in June 1883 to connect the Scarborough & Whitby Railway, which was then in the course of construction, to the N.E.R. lines at Scarborough. Further details about the history of Gallows Close can be found in the author's two books on the Scarborough & Whitby Railway.

63. North Eastern Railway Parcels Van, number 11, with the driver Mr John Lightfoot who died, aged only 36, in 1910. He had worked for the railway all his life in the Scarborough district.

Mrs Sybil Hall Collection.

64. British Railways standard class 3 engine, 77004, at work in Gallows Close goods yard on 10 January 1962. In the centre, behind the engine, can be seen the Roscoe Street Coal Depot, and on the left, Gladstone Road schools.

Fred Rowntree.

65. Mr E. Layton, Goods Agent in charge of Gallows Close, with the new Mechanical Horse which started to take over from the four-legged variety in the 1930s.

Jack Layton Collection.

66. This former L.M.S. 'Jinty' engine was stationed at Scarborough for a few years and is seen here acting as goods yard pilot. This unusual view was taken from the south-west end of Wykeham Street bridge.

John Williams.

67. The Mayor of Scarborough, Councillor Miles Bird J.P., presenting a Safe Driving Award to goods motor driver W. Mason in Gallows Close goods yard.

Jack Layton Collection.

68. Another view of Bertram Mills Circus (see photograph 26) detraining, this time at Gallows Close where a tractor carefully removes a long van off a flat wagon.

Fred Rowntree.

69. The turntable at the north end of the carriage sidings, built for the excursion trains from Londesborough Road station, where class J25, 65663, turns after arriving on the Whitby Pickup Goods on 6 August 1954.

Norman Skinner.

ACCIDENTS and INCIDENTS

Over the years a great variety of accidents and incidents have occurred on the railway at Scarborough, as might be expected at a busy terminal station. These have ranged from relatively minor events, such as causing an engine to emit too much smoke, to more serious matters involving collisions with engines or rolling stock. With one exception fatal accidents, which have fortunately been few and far between, have not involved major loss of life.

The punishments meted out by the railway company ranged from just a simple caution to fines, reduction of pay, suspension and, at the worst, dismissal from the service of the company. Many of the incidents at Scarborough were recorded in the N.E.R. *Registers of Enginemen & Firemen* which were rescued by Ken Hoole some years ago. Some extracts, relating to the staff at Scarborough, are reproduced here to illustrate that the lives of the drivers and firemen were not always happy ones although some incidents did have their humorous sides. The names have been shortened to initials to save any embarrassment!

Starting with the minor incidents the following only received a caution for their various misdemeanours – S.S. had engine 1503 off the rails through inattention to the turntable in 1890; G.T., a driver stationed at Whitby, caused a collision between engines 534 and 436 on 14 December 1904; J.W.J., a Scarborough driver, had engine 1524 short of steam at Falsgrave, delaying the 1-45 p.m. York to Scarborough on 28 August 1901 – so near yet so far! G.H. caused a smoke nuisance with engine 1541 on 24 July 1905; M.B. allowed engine 2026 to collide with empty carriages during shunting operations in No. 9 platform line on 27 January 1910, he also caused damage to a Great Eastern Railway wagon by allowing engine 1200 to collide with it on 2 December 1925; W.N. caused damage to be done to a can of milk through not having observed the condition of the brake tap on engine 1431 on 3 July 1909; and J.W.S., a fireman at Scarborough, ran engine 416 through a pair of points at the station without a signal on 20 July 1900, he also received a caution for coming late on duty twice.

70. This N.E.R. class W engine is thought to be number 690 which is recorded as passing a signal at danger and running through trap points at Falsgrave sidings on 27 August 1913. The driver was suspended for a day.

Author's Collection.

71. (right) New Manor Road bridge (now commonly called Woodland Ravine bridge) after an enemy aircraft dropped a bomb, in 1941, which landed behind the southeast abutment. The resulting explosion blew the abutment across the tracks and a lady pushing a pram across the bridge was tragically killed. The tracks were slewed round the obstruction and normal service was restored within a few days.

Author's Collection.

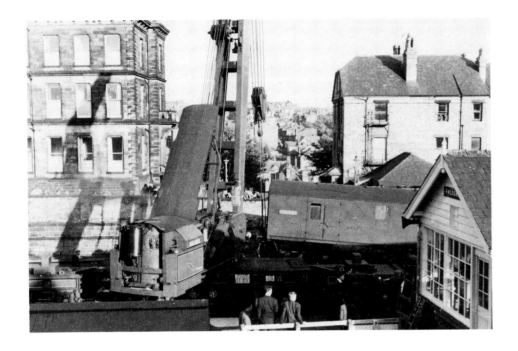

The following staff were fined for their actions – M.B. 2/6d for omitting to take the single line tablet at Falsgrave tunnel when working the 10-32 a.m. train to Saltburn on 25 August 1906; W.B., also 2/6d, for having his engine off the line at Falsgrave cabin in January 1880. J.W., a driver stationed at Scarborough, was fined a hefty 10/- (50p) in September 1886 for running past a signal and colliding with carriages. By way of a surprising contrast, G.H. was only fined 1/6d for using a hammer and chisel to open the sight feed lubricator tap of engine 1330 which resulted in the steam cock being broken off and the failure of the engine on 4 November 1905.

The following were suspended for their more serious offences – G.H., two weeks, for mistaking a signal and running engine 1535 through a pair of points on 30 January 1899; W.N. was suspended for one month for allowing a passenger to ride on his engine from York to Scarborough on 12 November 1898. G.B. was suspended for six days after failing to come on duty on three days during one April, and a further note records that he left the service and emigrated to Canada – to evade the law!

A number of accidents were caused by the special problems of working trains in and out of a terminal station where, if the engine hauls its coaches into the station it becomes trapped until the coaches are hauled out by the 'passenger pilot' engine. At Scarborough it was at one time the practice to stop the trains outside the station, detach the engines, which would run round the coaches, so that they could be propelled into the station. This resulted in so many accidents (on one occasion, in 1891, 38 passengers were injured) that the practice of propelling into the station was discontinued.

One incident, which happened to a member of the locomotive shed staff, occurred when he went with a train-load of local football supporters to watch Scarborough play Ossett Albion in 1962. Scarborough won but one of the opposing supporters struck him with the handbell he used to celebrate every time the away team scored!

72. (above left) On 13 May 1964 an errant parcels van became derailed opposite Falsgrave signal box and is seen here being put back on the straight and narrow by a rail-mounted crane. Services into Scarborough were terminated at Seamer and passengers transferred by bus.

Fred Rowntree.

73. (left) The driver of this Diesel Multiple Unit, on 26 June 1960, was obviously expecting to run right in to Scarborough station and the shortness of platform 1A must have taken him by surprise.

Ken Hoole.

SIGNAL BOXES

Before the introduction of signal boxes trains were worked, in the early days, on the time interval system. Policemen were stationed at level crossings and junctions to control the passage of trains and they were the forerunners of the signalmen. The time interval system was an unsafe method of working and resulted in many serious accidents.

It is recorded that in 1871 there were only two signalboxes at Scarborough and these were manned round the clock by four signalmen. Three of the signalmen were crippled – one had lost an arm, one a leg, and the other, part of a foot. The hours of duty were 6-00 a.m. to 6-00 p.m. and 6-00 p.m. to 6-00 a.m. Block signalling had not come into operation by 1871 and trains were still being worked by the time interval system. There were nine trains each way on the York line and six on the Hull line, each day.

Scarborough eventually had six signal boxes, all of which are illustrated on the following pages. The most interesting record book, from a signal box, is the *Occurrence Book* in which the signalman had to record every accident and incident which happened in the area controlled by his box. Fortunately a few of the books have survived for Scarborough including ones from 'Gallows Close' and 'Gasworks' and the following are just a few of the more interesting entries -

'GASWORKS'

27 August 1955 – Engine 77013, which worked the 10-49 a.m. arrival from Darlington, caused slight damage to holdup points behind the cabin at 11-20 a.m. Ganger Baker called for 11-45 to 1-45 p.m.

1 April 1956 – Leeds to Scarborough train long time in section, 12-34 to 12-50, engine 61240. Child having fallen from train – Ambulance met train on arrival. Driver off engine 61110 reported all clear.

9 July 1957 – Owing to the York to Scarborough Pickup (Goods) being in section for a long time between Seamer East and Gasworks signal boxes I stopped and cautioned the Scarborough to Bradford Diesel trial train through the section at 2-38 p.m.

7 February 1958 – Unable to open box at 8 a.m. as signals were frozen in the off position. Signals released at 11 a.m., box opened same time.

16 March 1959 – Engine 61259 derailed at Shed entrance. Engines worked in and out Gasworks outlet from 6-50 a.m.

29 March 1959 – Station Inspector reported a lineside fire near Quartons greenhouses 12-29 p.m. Ganger Baker called out. Under control 2-30 p.m.

4 June 1960 – Received 'Stop and Examine' ex-Washbeck 3-27 p.m. for Empty Coaching Stock train 3-10 p.m. Scarborough to York. Handbrake hard on in rear van. Attended to here, departed 3-33 p.m.

74. 'Scarborough' signal box was built in the early years of this century when platforms 6, 7, 8 and 9 were provided to cope with the increased passenger traffic. When the station was reduced back to five platforms in the 1980s this box was demolished and control was transferred to 'Falsgrave'.
Ken Mills.

75. Another view of 'Scarborough' box and its environs in 1965. Space inside the box was very cramped although an original drawing for a signal box here shows one with a narrower ground floor section.
Frank Dean.

76. Prior to 1908 the signal box at Falsgrave was situated on the south side of the tracks. This was one of Scarborough's two original signal boxes (the other was near Washbeck) which were erected by 1871. The train is being hauled by N.E.R. class M1, 1629, which was built in 1893.

Peter Cooper Collection.

77. The second Falsgrave box was built on the north side of the tracks, near the tunnel. At that time platform 1 ended some distance short of 'Falsgrave' box but in 1934 it was extended and the 1A bay platform built in front of the box. Originally it had 120 levers, the largest signal box in Scarborough.

Ken Hoole.

78. 'Washbeck' signal box was situated between Londesborough Road station and the locomotive yard. The design was almost identical to that of 'Falsgrave' box with its central projecting balcony. It was built in 1908 to control the entrance to the excursion station.

Doug Hardy.

79. 'Gasworks' signal box was situated near the south end of the locomotive yard (see photograph 34). It was extended in 1908 in conjunction with the opening of Londesborough Road station. This box controlled access to the Gasworks and 'Gas Down' carriage sidings.

Norman Skinner.

'GALLOWS CLOSE'

28 May 1930 – Coupling hook between wagon and van of York Goods broke, train brought to a stand at Washbeck, wagon standing at my end of tunnel in sight. Pilot engine propelled van to train and recoupled, departing at 5-25.

15 August 1931 – Informed by Ganger Hodgson that sewer main had burst under Manor Road bridge at 5-40 p.m. and rail on lower side was under water, all trains cautioned. *And the trouble continued* – on 20 August – 4-50 p.m. Ganger Hodgson says all trains had better be cautioned as up line between Manor Road and Hibernia Street bridges were under water owing to sewer main burst.

19 August 1935 – Considerable disorganisation and delay was caused to a passenger train and the York Goods when the signalman at Falsgrave asked the signalman at Gallows Close if he would accept the pilot loco with three wagons. Thinking that he could quickly get the short train into a siding in the goods yard he accepted and was somewhat startled and displeased to see the pilot emerge from Falsgrave tunnel hauling no less than 54 wagons!

A serious conflagration was avoided on 13 September 1935 when an L.M.S. wagon containing straw caught fire in the goods yard whilst Sentinel engine 198 was shunting. The driver had the great presence of mind, with the help of the shunters, to run the wagon under the water crane at the southwest end of Wykeham Street bridge where the fire was quickly extinguished.

80. (above right) 'Gallows Close' signal box was similar, in design, to 'Gasworks' box but shorter in length with only 3 arched windows on the ground floor as opposed to six. This is the second box in Gallows Close, the first was situated on the south side of Wykeham Street bridge adjacent to the Roscoe Street coal depot and was a much smaller structure in use before the development of the goods yard in the 1890s.

Alan Brown.

81. (right) 'Weaponess' was a tiny signal cabin, as seen here, and was only open during the summer months. It was installed to divide the long stretch of track between 'Gasworks' and 'Seamer East' into two block sections in order to accommodate a greater density of traffic on the approach lines into Scarborough during the busy summer seasons. The box closed in 1939 although the photograph was not taken until 25 May 1952, shortly before it was demolished.

J. W. Armstrong.

STATIONMASTERS and STAFF

Scarborough's first stationmaster is thought to have been Mr T. Mennell who impressed the fireman at the opening of the line who recalled, in later years, that he was a stoutly built man. A full list of the stationmasters here, down to 1982, is as follows –

T. Mennell	1845 - 1866
H. Grover	1866 - 1870
J. Bearup	1870 - 1882
W. Taylor	1882 - 1890
G. Brown	1890 - 1912
A. Horsley	1912 - 1922
F. W. Dowson	1922 - 1943
H. Baines	1944 - 1946
J. C. Handley	1946 - 1948
E. Brookes	1948 - 1954
W. A. A. Scott	1954 - 1957
A. Maleham	1957 - 1959
J. F. Layton	1959 - 1982

Records from the early years are sparse and the first stationmaster for whom any extensive details have survived is John Bearup. He was born in Newcastle in 1828 and apprenticed to a master butcher in 1842. He was married at York in 1857 and his occupation was given as railway inspector. He was resident in Scarborough in 1861 and became stationmaster in 1870. In 1882 he took over the Station Hotel which he managed for thirteen years. He was reputed to have distilled his own whisky but whether this activity was undertaken at Scarborough station is not recorded!

82. Frederick Dowson was one of Scarborough's longest serving stationmasters being appointed in 1922 and retiring at the end of 1943. Mr Dowson commenced his service with the North Eastern Railway Company as a clerk at Sandsend, near Whitby, when he was only 13 years old. He then served at Nunthorpe, Staithes and Loftus before working in the booking office at Scarborough in 1901. He then went to York as Relief Clerk, was appointed Train Inspector there in 1912 and then Assistant Stationmaster in June 1920. He transferred to Scarborough, as Stationmaster, in May 1922. The popularity of Mr Dowson, both amongst the staff and in the local community, can be judged from the fact that there were 200 guests at a reception to mark his silver wedding anniversary.

Author's Collection.

One of the best sources of information on the staff is in the pages of the railway company magazines – North Eastern Railway (starting in 1911), L.N.E.R. and British Railways (up to 1963). The author has extracted all the names, details and dates of the staff who are recorded as working on the railway at Scarborough from 1911 to 1963. Some of the memories recalled by the staff make fascinating reading and some are recorded in the following paragraphs.

Mr E. Green, 80 years old in 1928, recalled early years at Scarborough – 'I fired engine 180 which took King Edward to Scarborough, where he was taken ill, in the autumn of 1869. Number 180 was a single-wheeler and, like all N.E.R. locos of the time, burned coke. I very often fired the King's train between Scarborough and York or Beverley where he used to shoot as guest of Lord Londesborough. I had him as often as five days in one week and they were good days for us. His Lordship saw that we didn't go short of food, his tips were golden, and we usually came in for a couple of rabbits or a bit of game, but his strict instructions were, "No beer for those enginemen"!'

'We only had handbrakes in my early days. We often had to follow a fish train out of Scarborough on the way to York – a fish train dropping herring grease on the rails all the way. The rails were so slippery that we couldn't pull up properly at the roadside stations. We overran the platforms and couldn't set back with single-wheeled engines and no back-sanding arrangements. Passengers and porters, loaded with far more luggage than people carry about nowadays, had to scamper up to the train and scramble in as best they could. These were in the days of small brake vans, when luggage was strapped on to the top of the coaches and sheeted.'

In 1935 Tindall Bowman of Malton wrote a letter to Fred Dowson, stationmaster at Scarborough, in which he recalled his memories of the station in the 1870s: Staff at the station in 1871 – Stationmaster John Bearup, one Assistant Stationmaster, a Foreman Porter, six guards, one ticket collector, 14 porters, four signalmen and two policemen. Wages in 1873 – Stationmaster £2-13s-10d (£2.69), Assistants £1-8s-0d (£1.40) and £1-4s-0d (£1.20) (two at this time), Porters 18/- (90p), first year of service 17/- (85p).

83. (above right) A group of fifty-one station staff, at Scarborough, in L.N.E.R. days, including the stationmaster, Fred Dowson, in the middle of the second row. In 1891 there were over 120 staff employed at the station.

Derek Barker Collection.

84. (right) Stationmaster Fred Dowson presenting Safe Driving awards to some of the Scarborough staff. The Road Motor, or Mechanical Horse as it was often called, was used extensively to collect and deliver goods, parcels and 'passenger luggage in advance'.

Author's Collection.

85. The L.N.E.R. established its first staff training school at Scarborough, in 1942, in a buffet car which can be seen here, with the students, at platform 9 on the south side of the station.
Author's Collection.

An old ledger kept at Scarborough Goods recorded the names and details of every employee in the goods yard from 1870. The book was started by Mr Henry Mutch Horsley who began work at Scarborough goods yard in 1862 as a junior clerk earning £15 a year. The book records that the lowest paid employee started as a telegraph clerk at 2/6d (13p) a week in 1877. Another man, who had been a farm servant, a common source of labour for the railways, started at 18/- (90p) a week in 1873. It took the clerk twelve years to catch up with the farm labourer. By contrast the Chief Goods Agent's salary in 1898 was £300 a year. One of the staff, another former farm servant, had joined the railway in 1856, at the age of 26, so had been born in 1830 before any of the local railways had been built. Amongst the names recorded in the ledger there was a porter in 1878 called George Stephenson, whilst, more recently, there was a Mr R. Rocket on the staff.

Long hours of duty were the order of the day before 1900. In the *Scarborough Passenger Summer Staff Arrangements 1893* leaflet, Assistant Stationmaster Fred Jarvis was rostered to take duty from 5-30 a.m. to 7-40 p.m. with 40 minutes for breakfast, one hour for dinner (lunch) and no tea interval in spite of an overall shift of 14 hours and 10 minutes every day. Clerks worked a mere 13 hours and signalmen were instructed to take 'meals in cabins'.

Many railway staff volunteered their services in World War One and one, who served with the Yorkshire Hussars, managed to keep his sense of humour under trying circumstances as is illustrated in a short quotation from one of his letters – 'It is glorious weather here, and I am in the best of spirits but give me the Alexandra Gardens and the Fol-de-Rols anytime before Ypres. I booked a front seat at the last named spot and, after a continuous performance of three days, came away with a bit of shrapnel in my hand'.

Because of the shortage of experienced male clerks, in World War Two the L.N.E.R. established its first staff training school at Scarborough. This was in a buffet car, conveniently placed at the passenger station (see photograph 85), which was opened on 13 July 1942. The coach was used as a classroom and the students resided at a boarding house in the town. Students stayed for a month and tuition

86. (left) The North Eastern Railway Cottage Homes movement was formed in 1920, in the interests of the welfare of the railway staff, and by the time these houses were opened at Scarborough on 29 September 1923 they had already erected 40 with the prospect of completing 70 by the end of the financial year. The Cottage Homes Committee had also spent £6000 in helping members in time of need. These homes at Scarborough were opened by the Chairman of the new London & North Eastern Railway Company, Mr William Whitelaw, and it was thought to be his first public appearance in the North Eastern Area.
Author's Collection.

hours were from 8-45 a.m. to 5-15 p.m. with one hour for 'prep' most evenings. The counter in the buffet car was furnished with ticket rack, parcels weigh, rate books, reference books, account books and various forms – in effect it was fitted up to represent a small station. The number attending each course was limited to twenty.

The following amusing story was recalled by Fred Dowson as typical of some of the strange things that happened to passengers – once an embarrassed traveller got off the train from York and asked to speak to him privately. He then explained that, when using the toilet, he had coughed and his dentures had gone down the toilet. He could only estimate the time when it happened, not the place. Fred Dowson assured him he would work out the approximate place and ask the platelayers to keep a lookout for them. A few days later he asked the traveller to call and collect the dentures. The grateful traveller naturally enquired where they had been found. Mr Dowson smiled and told him – near Spitall level crossing!

87. (above right) The arrival of Father Christmas at Scarborough station. Far from coming by train from the North Pole it would have shattered a few young dreams if they had known that Santa changed into his outfit in the train toilet at Seamer! The first time that he arrived by 600 horse power diesel was in December 1962.

L. Dobson.

88. (right) When Jack Layton became stationmaster at Scarborough in 1959 he was said to be the youngest stationmaster ever appointed here. He was born in Darlington in 1925, during the centenary celebrations of the Stockton & Darlington Railway, and, as he admits, a railway career was almost pre-ordained with such an auspicious start. He commenced his career at Forge Valley station, on the Pickering line, in 1941 when his father was goods agent at Gallows Close. He served at many stations in the district including most of those between here and York. After four years in the service of his country he took up his career again at Thornton Dale and, after passing competitive examinations to become a traffic apprentice, he held responsible posts at Leeds, York, Hull and Stockton. It was always his ambition to return to Scarborough, which he accomplished in 1959, but this was not an easy post – he recalled that in about 1960 Scarborough station handled 800,000 passengers, a quarter of them in August alone. On Bank Holiday Saturday in 1961 there were 138 trains in and out of the station. Jack Layton was also Scarborough's last stationmaster as the post was redesignated station manager after he retired. This photograph was taken on his last day at the station on 16 November 1982.

Scarborough Evening News.

89. N.E.R. Royal Mail coach 291 standing in the station goods yard in about 1900. By 1912 the N.E.R. had nine Mail Vans. During the summer months a Travelling Post Office ran between York and Scarborough and old postcards and letters can be found with the cancellation – 'York & Scarbro TPO'.

Author's Collection.

90. The York–Scarborough line was frequently used as a test track for vehicles fresh out of York Carriage Works. This coach, standing adjacent to Londesborough Road station, is an ex-L.N.E.R. Travelling Post Office which had been rebuilt at York.

Fred Rowntree.

91. N.E.R. Petrol Inspection Car, 3711, was powered by a four-cylinder engine which covered 12 miles to the gallon. It was built in 1908 and could carry up to eight people. The photograph shows the vehicle standing at platform 1A.

Author's Collection.

92. All the lines in the area were regularly inspected by the District Engineer and his staff who were conveyed, in some comfort and style in L.N.E.R. and B.R. days, in Inspection Saloons like this, photographed in Gallows Close.

Ken Hoole.

THE DIESEL ERA

In the search for economy the railway companies have experimented with various forms of traction, over the years, in order to minimise running and maintenance costs. The first attempts on these lines were made by the North Eastern Railway Company in the early years of the century when they utilised elderly tank locomotives, including the 'BTP' class (photograph 44), which were semi-permanently coupled to specially built passenger coaches which had a driving

93. British Railways diesel, D2159, shunts a string of coal wagons at Scarborough Gasworks on 3 August 1964. This was a largely neglected aspect of the railway scene at Scarborough but was captured by a photographer who was an acknowledged expert on the industrial railway scene.

Brian Webb.

94. (below) One of Scarborough's small diesel shunting engines, 03.113, performs an unusual and mammoth task in hauling the Filey Holiday Camp to Glasgow excursion in July 1975. In order to release the train engine for its working out of Scarborough it was detached and the train was hauled in by this diminutive shunter.

Fred Rowntree.

95. (below right) The closure of the steam locomotive depot in 1963 led to scenes like this in the loco yard – D53 and D6809 replacing the steam locomotives of a few years earlier.

David Bointon.

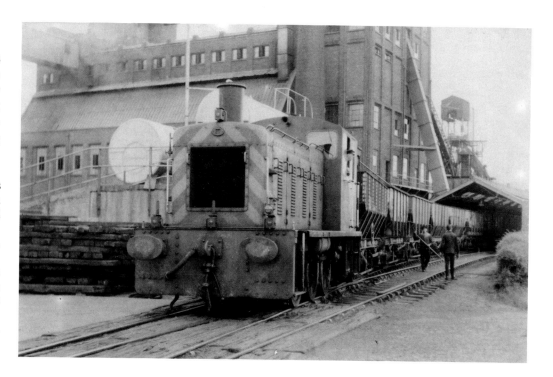

compartment at one end. This enabled the trains (Autocars) to be driven from either end and improved efficiency on local branch lines. Also at the beginning of the century the N.E.R. operated two petrol-electric railcars which ran between Scarborough and Filey from about 1904–1908.

The L.N.E.R. ran a diesel-electric railcar, *Tyneside Venturer,* which operated out of Scarborough in the winter months and was also used on a circular tour, Scarborough - Pickering - Whitby - Scarborough, during the summer. In 1928 the company introduced Sentinel–Cammell steam railcars (photograph 37) which eventually ran in a distinctive green and cream livery and were named after stage

96. (left) Two English Electric Type 1 engines, D8067 and D8058 haul in an Elsecar to Scarborough relief train on 22 August 1964.

Fred Rowntree.

97. (below left) Steam is dead, long live steam! Class 108/1, E50638, on the 16-07 Scarborough to York on 13 August 1978, gives a good impression of a steam locomotive almost on the 10th anniversary of the end of steam traction on British Rail.

Ken Mills.

98. (below) The first Sprinter in Scarborough departs promptly on the 09-54 to York. The double roof in this photograph is that of the original station of 1845 – platform 3 was the original arrival platform.

Robin Lidster.

coaches. These were moderately successful and lasted for about twenty years.

British Railways continued with the 'push-pull' idea, first introduced by the N.E.R. (photograph 51), but the greatest revolution in rail transport, on the local branch lines, came about in the late 1950s when Diesel Multiple Units (photograph 28) were introduced. They had many advantages over steam-hauled trains, requiring less major maintenance and servicing. They also became very popular with the travelling public as they were cleaner and gave better all-round visibility and, over short to medium distances, with frequent stops, gave a quicker service.

The first diesel locomotive hauled train, in Scarborough, arrived on 21 January 1960 with D252 which brought in a long test train of empty coaches from York. This heralded the end of the steam age at Scarborough, which had lasted 115 years, and ushered in the new diesel era.

100. (below) The first High Speed Train to visit Scarborough stands at platform 1 on Saturday 22 April 1978 prior to its departure to Edinburgh on a day trip organised by the Malton & Norton Lions Club. On the left Peter King, station supervisor, poses smartly for the press.

Robin Lidster.

101. (below right) The first HST again, this time the 'front' end with a pensive-looking young railway enthusiast who would just love to open that door!

Robin Lidster.

99. (above) The Royal Train, hauled by class 47, 527, brings H.R.H. Prince Charles to Scarborough in 1978.

Robin Lidster.

POSTSCRIPT: The future of Scarborough railway station can only be an uncertain one. If the Serpell Report of the early 1980s had been implemented the York – Scarborough line would already have been closed. As it is the current proposals to privatise the railways makes the retention of the less profitable lines unlikely. Whatever the future of the York – Scarborough line it is to be hoped that the undoubted architectural and historic merit of the buildings ensures the survival, with or without the railway, of Scarborough railway station.

102. Within a few years of the end of steam, on British Rail, special steam-hauled excursions were running into Scarborough. This photograph was taken on the notable occasion, on 16 June 1973, when two L.N.E.R. A4 class locomotives, *Bittern* and *Sir Nigel Gresley*, visited the town. The engines had to be sent out 'light' to turn on the triangle of track at Butlin's Holiday Camp station near Filey.

Fred Rowntree.

103. (below left) After the Butlin's triangle was lifted steam railway enthusiasts were delighted when it was announced that the turntable at the long-defunct former locomotive yard would be reinstated so that steam-hauled specials could be worked through from York. The old pit was dug out and it took three cranes to install the new turntable which was longer than the original and overlaps the edge of the pit. Unlike the original, which was pushed by hand, the new one was provided with a petrol engine to turn the locomotives.

Robin Lidster.

104. (below) The first locomotive to test the new turntable was this class 40 which appeared on 30 April 1981. The first 'Scarborough Spa Express' ran on Bank Holiday Monday, 25 May, and then on some Tuesdays and Wednesdays during July and August, between York and Scarborough. Nine different preserved steam locomotives, owned by the Steam Locomotive Operators' Association, were allocated to this service.

Adrian Scales.